MAD LIBS®

70s MAD LIBS

by Dan Alleva

MAD LIBS
An Imprint of Penguin Random House LLC, New York

Mad Libs format and text copyright © 2021 by Penguin Random House LLC.
All rights reserved.

Concept created by Roger Price & Leonard Stern

Cover illustration by Scott Brooks

Published by Mad Libs,
an imprint of Penguin Random House LLC, New York.
Printed in the USA.

Visit us online at www.penguinrandomhouse.com.

ISBN 9780593224113
1 3 5 7 9 10 8 6 4 2

MAD LIBS

INSTRUCTIONS

MAD LIBS® is a game for people who don't like games!
It can be played by one, two, three, four, or forty.

• RIDICULOUSLY SIMPLE DIRECTIONS

In this tablet you will find stories containing blank spaces where words
are left out. One player, the READER, selects one of these stories. The
READER does not tell anyone what the story is about. Instead, he/she asks
the other players, the WRITERS, to give him/her words. These words are
used to fill in the blank spaces in the story.

• TO PLAY

The READER asks each WRITER in turn to call out a word—an adjective or
a noun or whatever the space calls for—and uses them to fill in the blank
spaces in the story. The result is a MAD LIBS® game.

When the READER then reads the completed MAD LIBS® game to the other
players, they will discover that they have written a story that is fantastic,
screamingly funny, shocking, silly, crazy, or just plain dumb—depending
upon which words each WRITER called out.

• EXAMPLE (*Before* and *After*)

"_____!" he said _____
          EXCLAMATION   ADVERB

as he jumped into his convertible _____ and
                                             NOUN

drove off with his _____ wife.
                         ADJECTIVE

"_____**OUCH**_____!" he said _____**HAPPILY**_____
          EXCLAMATION   ADVERB

as he jumped into his convertible _____**CAT**_____ and
                                             NOUN

drove off with his _____**BRAVE**_____ wife.
                         ADJECTIVE

In case you have forgotten what adjectives, adverbs, nouns, and verbs are, here is a quick review:

An ADJECTIVE describes something or somebody. *Lumpy, soft, ugly, messy,* and *short* are adjectives.

An ADVERB tells how something is done. It modifies a verb and usually ends in "ly." *Modestly, stupidly, greedily,* and *carefully* are adverbs.

A NOUN is the name of a person, place, or thing. *Sidewalk, umbrella, bridle, bathtub,* and *nose* are nouns.

A VERB is an action word. *Run, pitch, jump,* and *swim* are verbs. Put the verbs in past tense if the directions say PAST TENSE. *Ran, pitched, jumped,* and *swam* are verbs in the past tense.

When we ask for A PLACE, we mean any sort of place: a country or city (*Spain, Cleveland*) or a room (*bathroom, kitchen*).

An EXCLAMATION or SILLY WORD is any sort of funny sound, gasp, grunt, or outcry, like *Wow!, Ouch!, Whomp!, Ick!,* and *Gadzooks!*

When we ask for specific words, like a NUMBER, a COLOR, an ANIMAL, or a PART OF THE BODY, we mean a word that is one of those things, like *seven, blue, horse,* or *head.*

When we ask for a PLURAL, it means more than one. For example, *cat* pluralized is *cats.*

MAD LIBS® is fun to play with friends, but you can also play it by yourself! To begin with, DO NOT look at the story on the page below. Fill in the blanks on this page with the words called for. Then, using the words you have selected, fill in the blank spaces in the story.

Now you've created your own hilarious MAD LIBS® game!

TIME TO BOOGIE DOWN WITH THE 70s

FIRST NAME _____

ADJECTIVE _____

NOUN _____

ADJECTIVE _____

PLURAL NOUN _____

VERB (PAST TENSE) _____

VERB _____

ADJECTIVE _____

NOUN _____

CITY _____

PLURAL NOUN _____

PLURAL NOUN _____

FIRST NAME _____

NOUN _____

ADJECTIVE _____

NOUN _____

ADJECTIVE _____

VERB ENDING IN "ING" _____

Hi, I'm _____ Savalas! I'm a TV host known for my
⟨FIRST NAME⟩

_____ catchphrase, "Who loves ya, _____?" The
⟨ADJECTIVE⟩   ⟨NOUN⟩

_____ _____ at Mad Libs _____ me
⟨ADJECTIVE⟩   ⟨PLURAL NOUN⟩   ⟨VERB (PAST TENSE)⟩

to introduce *70s Mad Libs*. So, what can I _____ to describe
⟨VERB⟩

how great the 70s were? They were _____, baby. But don't
⟨ADJECTIVE⟩

take my _____ for it—flip through the following pages. The
⟨NOUN⟩

70s is a decade known for many _____ celebrities like me,
⟨CITY⟩

but it was also an incredible decade for our athletic _____,
⟨PLURAL NOUN⟩

as they set out to prove who was the best of the _____
⟨PLURAL NOUN⟩

throughout sports. As for society in general, global icons like Mother

_____ won the Nobel Peace _____ in an era that
⟨FIRST NAME⟩   ⟨NOUN⟩

was very much defined by its _____ activism. And how
⟨ADJECTIVE⟩

could I forget disco??? It was such an amazing _____, I get
⟨NOUN⟩

_____ just _____ about it! Now, sit back and
⟨ADJECTIVE⟩   ⟨VERB ENDING IN "ING"⟩

enjoy *70s Mad Libs*!

MAD LIBS® is fun to play with friends, but you can also play it by yourself! To begin with, DO NOT look at the story on the page below. Fill in the blanks on this page with the words called for. Then, using the words you have selected, fill in the blank spaces in the story.

Now you've created your own hilarious MAD LIBS® game!

CELEBRITIES OF THE 70s

VERB ENDING IN "ING" _____

TYPE OF FOOD _____

TYPE OF LIQUID _____

FIRST NAME _____

PART OF THE BODY _____

NOUN _____

VERB ENDING IN "ING" _____

ADJECTIVE _____

ANIMAL _____

FIRST NAME _____

NOUN _____

LAST NAME _____

ADJECTIVE _____

PERSON IN ROOM _____

NOUN _____

PLURAL NOUN _____

VERB ENDING IN "ING" _____

Some celebrities of the 70s left a/an _____ impact on
VERB ENDING IN "ING"

future decades. Paul Newman was a movie star, but most people know

him today for his own brand of _____ and _____.
TYPE OF FOOD   TYPE OF LIQUID

Clint Eastwood portrayed the unforgettable Dirty _____, a
FIRST NAME

tough-_____ cop with a bad _____.
PART OF THE BODY   NOUN

These days, Clint does more _____ than acting,
VERB ENDING IN "ING"

and once had a very public, very _____ conversation
ADJECTIVE

with a chair. Pam Grier stunned audiences with her portrayal of the

title character in _____-y Brown! And we cannot forget
ANIMAL

Olivia Newton-_____, who starred in the timeless classic
FIRST NAME

_____ alongside John _____, the star of the
NOUN   LAST NAME

_____ TV series *Welcome Back,* _____.
ADJECTIVE   PERSON IN ROOM

Their duet "You're the _____ That I Want" topped the
NOUN

Billboard pop _____ list in 1978 and remains one of the
PLURAL NOUN

highest-_____ singles in history.
VERB ENDING IN "ING"

MAD LIBS® is fun to play with friends, but you can also play it by yourself! To begin with, DO NOT look at the story on the page below. Fill in the blanks on this page with the words called for. Then, using the words you have selected, fill in the blank spaces in the story.

Now you've created your own hilarious MAD LIBS® game!

ROCK 'N' ROLL IS ALIVE ON WPRH-AM RADIO

SILLY WORD _____

VERB _____

ADJECTIVE _____

FIRST NAME _____

A PLACE _____

COLOR _____

FIRST NAME _____

CITY _____

FIRST NAME _____

NUMBER _____

CELEBRITY _____

FIRST NAME _____

NOUN _____

ADJECTIVE _____

LAST NAME (PLURAL) _____

ARTICLE OF CLOTHING (PLURAL) _____

VERB _____

PLURAL NOUN _____

MAD LIBS®
ROCK 'N' ROLL IS ALIVE
ON WPRH-AM RADIO

Hey, everybody! It's DJ _____, coming live over the airwaves
SILLY WORD

on WPRH-AM, the station that has all your rock 'n' _____!
VERB

I tell you, folks, the phone lines are _____ hot with killer
ADJECTIVE

requests! There's _____ calling from (the) _____
FIRST NAME   A PLACE

wanting to hear some _____ Sabbath, and _____
COLOR   FIRST NAME

in _____, who tells me she can really get down with some
CITY

_____ Bowie, and our lucky caller number _____,
FIRST NAME   NUMBER

_____, who really wants to hear some Pink _____
CELEBRITY   FIRST NAME

tonight! And later, WPRH-AM has got all the juicy _____
NOUN

on the _____ punk-rock band the _____.
ADJECTIVE   LAST NAME (PLURAL)

Get this: They wear matching _____ and
ARTICLE OF CLOTHING (PLURAL)

sometimes _____ with one another onstage! Can you
VERB

imagine? Well, keep your _____ dialed to WPRH-AM to
PLURAL NOUN

hear all about it!

MAD LIBS® is fun to play with friends, but you can also play it by yourself! To begin with, DO NOT look at the story on the page below. Fill in the blanks on this page with the words called for. Then, using the words you have selected, fill in the blank spaces in the story.

Now you've created your own hilarious MAD LIBS® game!

70s BIRTHDAY WISH LIST

NOUN _____

ADJECTIVE _____

FIRST NAME _____

ANIMAL _____

VEHICLE _____

COLOR _____

ADJECTIVE _____

NUMBER _____

NOUN _____

PLURAL NOUN _____

VERB _____

NOUN _____

FIRST NAME _____

TYPE OF CONTAINER _____

PERSON IN ROOM _____

MAD LIBS®

70s BIRTHDAY WISH LIST

Dear Mom,

I've been a really good _____ this year, so I added some
                              NOUN

extra-_____ toys to my list:
          ADJECTIVE

1. A G.I. _____ action figure (first choice is the
                 FIRST NAME

   "_____ Eye" figure)
        ANIMAL

2. An Electric race _____ (please note: I prefer _____)
                         VEHICLE   COLOR

3. _____ Putty
        ADJECTIVE

4. A/An _____ *Million Dollar Man* action figure
             NUMBER

5. An Easy-Bake _____
                     NOUN

6. Lincoln _____
               PLURAL NOUN

7. A/An _____ Armstrong action figure
             VERB

8. An Atari _____ system
                 NOUN

9. A/An _____ -in-the-_____
             FIRST NAME   TYPE OF CONTAINER

Love,

_____
PERSON IN ROOM

MAD LIBS® is fun to play with friends, but you can also play it by yourself! To begin with, DO NOT look at the story on the page below. Fill in the blanks on this page with the words called for. Then, using the words you have selected, fill in the blank spaces in the story.

Now you've created your own hilarious MAD LIBS® game!

DEFINING SPORTS MOMENTS OF THE 70s

LETTER OF THE ALPHABET _____

VERB ENDING IN "ING" _____

FIRST NAME _____

NUMBER _____

ARTICLE OF CLOTHING _____

ADJECTIVE _____

PERSON IN ROOM _____

VERB ENDING IN "ING" _____

NUMBER _____

PLURAL NOUN _____

ADVERB _____

VERB (PAST TENSE) _____

ADJECTIVE _____

NOUN _____

VERB (PAST TENSE) _____

ADVERB _____

NOUN _____

MAD☺LIBS®
DEFINING SPORTS
MOMENTS OF THE 70s

Hey, sports fans! Here's ESP-_____'s defining
                                LETTER OF THE ALPHABET

sports moments of the 70s! Muhammad Ali was defeated by

"_____ _____" Frazier after _____
   VERB ENDING IN "ING"   FIRST NAME   NUMBER

rounds in 1971. Frazier wouldn't wear the heavyweight championship

_____ for long, though. He was defeated by
       ARTICLE OF CLOTHING

"_____ George" Foreman in 1973. Baseball legend Hank
      ADJECTIVE

Aaron broke _____'s home-run record on April 8, 1974,
              PERSON IN ROOM

by _____ home run number _____. As he
    VERB ENDING IN "ING"   NUMBER

rounded the _____, two students _____ jumped
              PLURAL NOUN   ADVERB

onto the field and _____ the bases alongside Aaron,
                      VERB (PAST TENSE)

a very _____ moment for the right fielder. Aaron held the
         ADJECTIVE

_____ for most home runs until 2007. Billie Jean King
    NOUN

_____ Bobby Riggs in the "Battle of the Sexes," a
   VERB (PAST TENSE)

famous tennis match. Sparked by comments Riggs made about female

tennis players, King beat Riggs _____ that day—a win
                                    ADVERB

seen as a boost not only for _____ but also for the women's
                                NOUN

liberation movement.

MAD LIBS® is fun to play with friends, but you can also play it by yourself! To begin with, DO NOT look at the story on the page below. Fill in the blanks on this page with the words called for. Then, using the words you have selected, fill in the blank spaces in the story.

Now you've created your own hilarious MAD LIBS® game!

ELECTRONICS SHACK

PLURAL NOUN _____

EXCLAMATION _____

ADJECTIVE _____

NOUN _____

VERB _____

ADJECTIVE _____

NUMBER _____

PLURAL NOUN _____

VERB _____

VERB (PAST TENSE) _____

PART OF THE BODY _____

ADJECTIVE _____

VERB _____

PART OF THE BODY _____

NUMBER _____

NOUN _____

VERB _____

VERB ENDING IN "ING" _____

Electronics Shack guarantees you'll find _____ you need
_____PLURAL NOUN_____

for a price that won't leave your wallet screaming, "_____!"
_____EXCLAMATION

Our items are cutting-edge—not _____ junk. We have
_____ADJECTIVE

the first pocket _____. Now you can add, subtract, and
_____NOUN

_____ numbers wherever you go! Need to make your life even
___VERB

more _____? We've got the Apple _____, the
_____ADJECTIVE_____NUMBER

personal computer for everyday use. Plus, we've got plenty of floppy

_____ to save your data! Are you always late? Does it
___PLURAL NOUN

_____ all your friends? Problem _____. We
___VERB_____VERB (PAST TENSE)

have a full selection of digital _____-watches that will
_____PART OF THE BODY

keep you on time. And all the _____-shots out there, we've
_____ADJECTIVE

got the very first cellular phones—phones so high-tech, you won't

_____ your _____! They may cost _____
___VERB_____PART OF THE BODY_____NUMBER

dollars and be as big as a/an _____, but you'll never
_____NOUN

_____ a call again! So, what are you _____
___VERB_____VERB ENDING IN "ING"

for? Come on down!

MAD LIBS® is fun to play with friends, but you can also play it by yourself! To begin with, DO NOT look at the story on the page below. Fill in the blanks on this page with the words called for. Then, using the words you have selected, fill in the blank spaces in the story.

Now you've created your own hilarious MAD LIBS® game!

BICENTENNIAL CELEBRATIONS

COUNTRY _____

TYPE OF EVENT (PLURAL) _____

SAME COUNTRY _____

ADJECTIVE _____

OCCUPATION (PLURAL) _____

NUMBER _____

VERB _____

VEHICLE _____

NUMBER _____

PLURAL NOUN _____

VERB (PAST TENSE) _____

PART OF THE BODY _____

COLOR _____

ARTICLE OF CLOTHING (PLURAL) _____

NUMBER _____

NOUN _____

OCCUPATION _____

ADJECTIVE _____

MAD LIBS
BICENTENNIAL CELEBRATIONS

_____'s Bicentennial was a series of _____
　　　COUNTRY　　　　　　　　　　　　　　　　　　　TYPE OF EVENT (PLURAL)

paying tribute to the events that led to the creation of _____
　　　　　　　　　　　　　　　　　　　　　　　　　SAME COUNTRY

as a/an _____ republic. The planning of the Bicentennial
　　　　　ADJECTIVE

began with _____ in Congress coming together
　　　　　　　OCCUPATION (PLURAL)

_____ years earlier to _____ the celebration.
　　NUMBER　　　　　　　　　　　　　VERB

On April 1, 1975, official events began, with the American Freedom

_____ departing from Delaware on a tour of the
　　　VEHICLE

_____ states, and for over a year, Bicentennial-themed
　　NUMBER

_____ were held across the nation. Many people
　　PLURAL NOUN

_____ from the sidewalks while others protested. The
　VERB (PAST TENSE)

Dallas Cowboys _____-ball team even wore red, white,
　　　　　　　　PART OF THE BODY

and _____ stripes on their _____ to
　　　COLOR　　　　　　　　　　ARTICLE OF CLOTHING (PLURAL)

celebrate. The Bicentennial celebrations concluded on July 4, 1976,

exactly _____ years after the adoption of the _____
　　　　　NUMBER　　　　　　　　　　　　　　　　　　NOUN

of Independence. As one _____ put it, the Bicentennial
　　　　　　　　　　　OCCUPATION

was a celebration of great patriotism and _____ memories.
　　　　　　　　　　　　　　　　　　　　ADJECTIVE

MAD LIBS® is fun to play with friends, but you can also play it by yourself! To begin with, DO NOT look at the story on the page below. Fill in the blanks on this page with the words called for. Then, using the words you have selected, fill in the blank spaces in the story.

Now you've created your own hilarious MAD LIBS® game!

WE'RE GOING TO DISNEY WORLD!

ADJECTIVE _____

ANIMAL _____

FIRST NAME _____

ADJECTIVE _____

PLURAL NOUN _____

NUMBER _____

VERB ENDING IN "ING" _____

NOUN _____

VERB (PAST TENSE) _____

ADJECTIVE _____

ADJECTIVE _____

A PLACE _____

VEHICLE _____

CELEBRITY _____

OCCUPATION _____

ADJECTIVE _____

PLURAL NOUN _____

MAD LIBS®

TALKING FILM

Here's *Talking Film*'s Top 10 Films of the 70s!

1. *The Godfather, Part* _____
   NUMBER

2. *Jaws*—Made audience members too _____ to
   ADJECTIVE

   _____ in the ocean!
   VERB

3. *The Texas Chain Saw* _____
   NOUN

4. *Taxi Driver*—A gritty and _____ movie!
   ADJECTIVE

5. _____ *Deadly Venoms*—Like slasher flicks, martial arts
   NUMBER

   movies were _____ during the 70s.
   ADJECTIVE

6. _____ *and the Holy Grail*—It's the _____ Grail
   CELEBRITY   ADJECTIVE

   of British cinema!

7. *Shaft's Big* _____!
   NOUN

8. *Chinatown*—Jack Nicholson is a/an _____ in this
   OCCUPATION

   neo-noir essential.

9. *The Exorcist*— _____ will never look the same after you
   TYPE OF FOOD

   watch Linda Blair _____ it flying!
   VERB

10. *Apocalypse* _____—A/An _____ portrait of the
    ADVERB   ADJECTIVE

    Vietnam War.

MAD LIBS® is fun to play with friends, but you can also play it by yourself! To begin with, DO NOT look at the story on the page below. Fill in the blanks on this page with the words called for. Then, using the words you have selected, fill in the blank spaces in the story.

Now you've created your own hilarious MAD LIBS® game!

SCANDAL!

ADJECTIVE _____

FIRST NAME _____

PLURAL NOUN _____

ADJECTIVE _____

COUNTRY _____

OCCUPATION _____

VERB ENDING IN "ING" _____

TYPE OF LIQUID _____

VERB _____

NOUN _____

VERB _____

VERB ENDING IN "ING" _____

ADJECTIVE _____

FIRST NAME _____

VERB (PAST TENSE) _____

COLOR _____

TYPE OF BUILDING _____

NOUN _____

MAD LIBS®

SCANDAL!

The year 1972 was a/an _____ time for politics. President
_____ADJECTIVE_____

_____ M. Nixon faced _____ in response to
____FIRST NAME____   ____PLURAL NOUN____

the Vietnam War, viewed as _____ by many Americans.
_____ADJECTIVE_____

Early that year, Nixon visited _____ , becoming the first
_____COUNTRY_____

sitting _____ to visit the region, ending twenty-five
____OCCUPATION____

years of the two nations not _____ with each
_____VERB ENDING IN "ING"_____

other. However, it all came crashing down for the president when the

_____ -gate scandal rocked the nation, forcing Nixon
____TYPE OF LIQUID____

to _____ . Nixon famously said, "I am not a/an
____VERB____

_____ ," but the damage had already been done. People felt
____NOUN____

they could no longer _____ what was _____
_____VERB_____   ____VERB ENDING IN "ING"____

in government. It was a/an _____ day for democracy, but
____ADJECTIVE____

also for _____ Presley, who once _____
____FIRST NAME____   ____VERB (PAST TENSE)____

with Nixon at the _____ _____ . There's even
____COLOR____   ____TYPE OF BUILDING____

a famous photo of the pair taken together in the Oval _____ .
____NOUN____

MAD LIBS® is fun to play with friends, but you can also play it by yourself! To begin with, DO NOT look at the story on the page below. Fill in the blanks on this page with the words called for. Then, using the words you have selected, fill in the blank spaces in the story.

Now you've created your own hilarious MAD LIBS® game!

DISCO DAD

ADJECTIVE _____

ARTICLE OF CLOTHING (PLURAL) _____

ADJECTIVE _____

PLURAL NOUN _____

NUMBER _____

VERB (PAST TENSE) _____

ADJECTIVE _____

CELEBRITY _____

FIRST NAME _____

VERB ENDING IN "ING" _____

EXCLAMATION _____

PLURAL NOUN _____

OCCUPATION _____

NOUN _____

NUMBER _____

PART OF THE BODY (PLURAL) _____

PLURAL NOUN _____

ADJECTIVE _____

MAD LIBS®

DISCO DAD

This is the most _____ song ever, son! It's called "Boogie
           ADJECTIVE

_____." The disco era was a/an _____
ARTICLE OF CLOTHING (PLURAL)   ADJECTIVE

time. Besides music and fashion, the scene promoted unity among

_____ of all backgrounds. Your mother and I would go to
PLURAL NOUN

this club, Studio _____ . If you were _____
          NUMBER   VERB (PAST TENSE)

there, people thought you were somebody _____ .
                                    ADJECTIVE

_____ or _____ Warhol could be
   CELEBRITY   FIRST NAME

seen there on any given night. People on the dance floor would be

_____ the chorus of "Le Freak" by Chic, shouting,
VERB ENDING IN "ING"

"Ahhhhhhhhhhh, _____!" We'd all do the hustle as
                  EXCLAMATION

_____ lit up the dance floor. "Dancing _____"
PLURAL NOUN   OCCUPATION

by ABBA was another great song, but "Heart of _____" by
                                    NOUN

Blondie topped the charts for like _____ weeks. Boy, we used
                             NUMBER

to sing and dance our _____ off! Your mother and
                    PART OF THE BODY (PLURAL)

I may have been just _____ back then, but we partied
                    PLURAL NOUN

until we were _____!
         ADJECTIVE

MAD LIBS® is fun to play with friends, but you can also play it by yourself! To begin with, DO NOT look at the story on the page below. Fill in the blanks on this page with the words called for. Then, using the words you have selected, fill in the blank spaces in the story.

Now you've created your own hilarious MAD LIBS® game!

FASHION FLASHBACK WITH MOM

ADVERB _____

NOUN _____

CELEBRITY _____

ARTICLE OF CLOTHING (PLURAL) _____

NOUN _____

TYPE OF CONTAINER _____

ANIMAL _____

PART OF THE BODY _____

ADJECTIVE _____

ADVERB _____

VERB ENDING IN "ING" _____

ADJECTIVE _____

PERSON IN ROOM _____

ARTICLE OF CLOTHING _____

LAST NAME _____

NUMBER _____

ARTICLE OF CLOTHING _____

ADJECTIVE _____

MAD LIBS®

THE TV GUIDE

Here's a rundown of my _____ 70s TV programming:
                        ADJECTIVE

8 a.m.—*CBS Morning News* with _____ and *Gourmet*
                                   CELEBRITY

_____
VERB ENDING IN "ING"

10 a.m.—*School-*_____ *Rock!* and _____ *and*
                    TYPE OF BUILDING   PERSON IN ROOM

the Pussycats

12 p.m.—*The* _____ *Perry Mason* and *Starsky &*
                    ADJECTIVE

_____
LAST NAME

2 p.m.—*The New Adventures of* _____-*man* and *The*
                                      ANIMAL

Electric _____
              NOUN

4 p.m.—*The Rockford* _____ and *Land of the* _____
                          PLURAL NOUN   ADJECTIVE

7 p.m.— _____ *'s Angels*
              FIRST NAME

8 p.m.— _____ *Times* and *All in the* _____
              ADJECTIVE   NOUN

11 p.m.—*The Tonight Show Starring* _____ *Carson*
                                         FIRST NAME

MAD LIBS® is fun to play with friends, but you can also play it by yourself! To begin with, DO NOT look at the story on the page below. Fill in the blanks on this page with the words called for. Then, using the words you have selected, fill in the blank spaces in the story.

Now you've created your own hilarious MAD LIBS® game!

ACTIVISTS, PIONEERS, AND CRITICAL MOMENTS

ADJECTIVE _____

VERB _____

PLURAL NOUN _____

NOUN _____

VERB ENDING IN "ING" _____

COUNTRY _____

ADJECTIVE _____

VERB (PAST TENSE) _____

ADJECTIVE _____

COUNTRY _____

CELEBRITY _____

VERB _____

NOUN _____

VERB ENDING IN "ING" _____

OCCUPATION _____

VERB _____

ADJECTIVE _____

NOUN _____

MAD LIBS®
ACTIVISTS, PIONEERS, AND
CRITICAL MOMENTS

So many _____ events occurred in the 1970s: The Non-
          ADJECTIVE

Proliferation Treaty tried to stop the _____ of nuclear
                                        VERB

_____ . Gloria Steinem and others formed the National
PLURAL NOUN

Women's Political Caucus, a non- _____ group supporting
                                  NOUN

women _____ for office. Jane Fonda visited
        VERB ENDING IN "ING"

_____ , speaking against the United States' _____
COUNTRY   ADJECTIVE

policies in the region. Andy Warhol _____ his
                                      VERB (PAST TENSE)

_____ portrait of the communist leader of (the)
ADJECTIVE

_____ , _____ . Barbara Walters became the first
COUNTRY   CELEBRITY

woman to co- _____ on *The Today Show*. Beverly Johnson
              VERB

became the first African American woman to be featured on the

_____ of *Vogue*. Tennis icon Arthur Ashe defeated the
NOUN

_____ champion, Jimmy Connors, to become the first
VERB ENDING IN "ING"

African American to ever win at Wimbledon. Harvey Milk was elected

as the first openly gay _____ in the history of California.
                         OCCUPATION

And hip- _____ was born, launching a/an _____
          VERB   ADJECTIVE

musical _____ across the globe.
         NOUN

MAD LIBS® is fun to play with friends, but you can also play it by yourself! To begin with, DO NOT look at the story on the page below. Fill in the blanks on this page with the words called for. Then, using the words you have selected, fill in the blank spaces in the story.

Now you've created your own hilarious MAD LIBS® game!

THE FIRST EARTH DAY

PERSON IN ROOM _____

ADJECTIVE _____

VERB ENDING IN "ING" _____

NOUN _____

A PLACE _____

PLURAL NOUN _____

ADVERB _____

ADJECTIVE _____

SAME PERSON IN ROOM _____

NOUN _____

TYPE OF LIQUID _____

NOUN _____

VERB (PAST TENSE) _____

PLURAL NOUN _____

NOUN _____

NOUN _____

FIRST NAME _____

MAD LIBS

THE FIRST EARTH DAY

Dear _____ ,
     PERSON IN ROOM

I hope this note finds you very _____ ! I'm
                                    ADJECTIVE

_____ you today because I wanted to see if you'd come
VERB ENDING IN "ING"

to an Earth Day _____ with me—the first of its kind—
                  NOUN

which is being held at my local _____ . A lot of the other
                              A PLACE

_____ from our school are going, _____ , and I
PLURAL NOUN   ADVERB

think it will be _____ . To be honest, _____ ,
            ADJECTIVE   SAME PERSON IN ROOM

I'm concerned about the state of our _____ . I'm worried
                              NOUN

about the raw _____ and toxic _____ that's being
             TYPE OF LIQUID   NOUN

_____ into our air and water. If someone doesn't say
VERB (PAST TENSE)

something now, then future _____ will suffer even more
                        PLURAL NOUN

than us. And it's during spring _____ , so you don't have to
                          NOUN

worry about missing _____ or anything!
                  NOUN

Anyway, let me know if you want to go!

Love,

_____
FIRST NAME

MAD LIBS® is fun to play with friends, but you can also play it by yourself! To begin with, DO NOT look at the story on the page below. Fill in the blanks on this page with the words called for. Then, using the words you have selected, fill in the blank spaces in the story.

Now you've created your own hilarious MAD LIBS® game!

"LIVE FROM NEW YORK..."

NOUN _____

ADJECTIVE _____

LAST NAME _____

NOUN _____

FIRST NAME _____

LAST NAME _____

ADJECTIVE _____

NOUN _____

LETTER OF THE ALPHABET _____

VERB ENDING IN "ING" _____

NOUN _____

OCCUPATION (PLURAL) _____

ADJECTIVE _____

TYPE OF FOOD (PLURAL) _____

OCCUPATION _____

NOUN _____

NUMBER _____

October 11, 1975—the date _Saturday_ _____ _Live_
NOUN

made its television debut. Led by _____ producer Lorne
ADJECTIVE

_____, the cast of _SNL_ was an all-_____
LAST NAME   NOUN

ensemble from the world of sketch comedy, starring comedians like

_____ Radner and John _____. They brought
FIRST NAME   LAST NAME

a/an _____ amount of comedic know-how to the cast.
ADJECTIVE

The show would develop a cult _____ among
NOUN

viewers of Generation _____. It's credited with
LETTER OF THE ALPHABET

_____ some of the best political commentary that
VERB ENDING IN "ING"

any _____ has ever offered, with its cast often impersonating
NOUN

_____ from elected offices. Some of _SNL_'s cast went on
OCCUPATION (PLURAL)

to have _____ movie careers. Bill Murray even starred in the
ADJECTIVE

1979 comedy _____, playing a/an _____
TYPE OF FOOD (PLURAL)   OCCUPATION

at Camp North _____. _SNL_ is still on the air today after
NOUN

_____ seasons.
NUMBER

MAD LIBS® is fun to play with friends, but you can also play it by yourself! To begin with, DO NOT look at the story on the page below. Fill in the blanks on this page with the words called for. Then, using the words you have selected, fill in the blank spaces in the story.

Now you've created your own hilarious MAD LIBS® game!

THE EPA RECOMMENDS . . .

NOUN _____

ADJECTIVE _____

VERB _____

NOUN _____

PLURAL NOUN _____

NOUN _____

ADJECTIVE _____

NOUN _____

VERB ENDING IN "ING" _____

ADJECTIVE _____

NUMBER _____

TYPE OF LIQUID _____

NOUN _____

A PLACE _____

ADJECTIVE _____

PLURAL NOUN _____

NOUN _____

A PLACE _____

MAD LIBS

THE EPA RECOMMENDS...

Since 1970, the Environmental _____ Agency has been
NOUN

setting _____ standards to _____ the _____.
ADJECTIVE   VERB   NOUN

Here are a few _____ the agency recommends:
PLURAL NOUN

1. Make sure your _____ isn't made of asbestos. That stuff
NOUN

   is a/an _____ _____!
   ADJECTIVE   NOUN

2. Traces of lead in your _____ water should never be
VERB ENDING IN "ING"

   tolerated, ever. That's why we created the _____ Water
   ADJECTIVE

   Act of 1972.

3. You may store no more than _____ containers of
NUMBER

   _____ in your home. Any more than that and you will
   TYPE OF LIQUID

   incur a/an _____, and perhaps even time in (the)
   NOUN

   _____.
   A PLACE

4. Always be _____ of _____ in the air. Your
ADJECTIVE   PLURAL NOUN

   local government has a/an _____ that monitors air
   NOUN

   quality in your _____.
   A PLACE

MAD LIBS® is fun to play with friends, but you can also play it by yourself! To begin with, DO NOT look at the story on the page below. Fill in the blanks on this page with the words called for. Then, using the words you have selected, fill in the blank spaces in the story.

Now you've created your own hilarious MAD LIBS® game!

ON THE MOVE IN THE 70s

VERB _____

ADJECTIVE _____

NUMBER _____

TYPE OF CONTAINER _____

NOUN _____

ADJECTIVE _____

OCCUPATION (PLURAL) _____

ANIMAL _____

VEHICLE _____

PLURAL NOUN _____

ADJECTIVE _____

NOUN _____

ADJECTIVE _____

NUMBER _____

NOUN _____

COUNTRY _____

A PLACE _____

ON THE MOVE IN THE 70s

There's so much ground to _____ regarding transportation
                              VERB
in the 70s. The decade began with the _____ rescue of
                                            ADJECTIVE
the crew of Apollo _____ in 1970. A damaged oxygen
                          NUMBER
_____ nearly caused a huge _____ on board.
TYPE OF CONTAINER   NOUN
Fortunately, the _____ expertise of the _____
                  ADJECTIVE   OCCUPATION (PLURAL)
at NASA saved the day. Back on Earth, the Ford _____
                                                    ANIMAL
muscle _____ tore up _____ everywhere
          VEHICLE   PLURAL NOUN
and was made popular in films and songs. But perhaps the most

_____ transportation development was the Concorde:
     ADJECTIVE
the _____ -powered, _____ -sonic passenger
        NOUN   ADJECTIVE
airliner. Its maximum speed was _____ times the
                                       NUMBER
_____ of sound, and because the planes were developed by
   NOUN
_____ and the United Kingdom, many are still on display
  COUNTRY
today throughout Europe in museums and aviation centers, as well as

in (the) _____ .
          A PLACE

From 70s MAD LIBS® • Copyright © 2021 by Penguin Random House LLC.

MAD LIBS® is fun to play with friends, but you can also play it by yourself! To begin with, DO NOT look at the story on the page below. Fill in the blanks on this page with the words called for. Then, using the words you have selected, fill in the blank spaces in the story.

Now you've created your own hilarious MAD LIBS® game!

THE FIRST TEST-TUBE BABY

PERSON IN ROOM _____

NOUN _____

VERB (PAST TENSE) _____

SILLY WORD _____

SAME PERSON IN ROOM _____

PART OF THE BODY _____

NUMBER _____

NOUN _____

VERB _____

NOUN _____

ADJECTIVE _____

NOUN _____

ADJECTIVE _____

SAME PERSON IN ROOM _____

ADJECTIVE _____

OCCUPATION (PLURAL) _____

NOUN _____

_____ is famous for being the first _____-tube
<u>PERSON IN ROOM</u>   <u>NOUN</u>

baby. Of course, there were no real test tubes involved—technically,

she was _____ in a special jar called a/an _____ .
    <u>VERB (PAST TENSE)</u>   <u>SILLY WORD</u>

Born in 1978, _____ was the first person born after
           <u>SAME PERSON IN ROOM</u>

being conceived outside the _____ . *Time* magazine called
              <u>PART OF THE BODY</u>

the event "the most awaited birth in perhaps _____ years,"
                 <u>NUMBER</u>

as reporters from around the _____ came to _____
          <u>NOUN</u>   <u>VERB</u>

this _____-breaking marvel of _____ science. At the
    <u>NOUN</u>   <u>ADJECTIVE</u>

time, the public _____ was mixed: Some claimed the occasion
         <u>NOUN</u>

was a celebration for would-be parents, while others protested that

scientists were heading down a/an _____ slope. Today,
                <u>ADJECTIVE</u>

_____ supports her parents' decision. She sees them
<u>SAME PERSON IN ROOM</u>

as _____ people, who were _____ in the
   <u>ADJECTIVE</u>   <u>OCCUPATION (PLURAL)</u>

_____-breaking study of in vitro fertilization.
<u>NOUN</u>

MAD LIBS® is fun to play with friends, but you can also play it by yourself! To begin with, DO NOT look at the story on the page below. Fill in the blanks on this page with the words called for. Then, using the words you have selected, fill in the blank spaces in the story.

Now you've created your own hilarious MAD LIBS® game!

THE LORDS OF SKATEBOARDING

VERB ENDING IN "ING" _____

ANIMAL _____

PLURAL NOUN _____

LETTER OF THE ALPHABET _____

NOUN _____

ADJECTIVE _____

NUMBER _____

VERB _____

ADJECTIVE _____

NOUN _____

PLURAL NOUN _____

NUMBER _____

ADJECTIVE _____

VERB _____

NOUN _____

VERB ENDING IN "ING" _____

ADJECTIVE _____

MAD LIBS®
THE LORDS OF SKATEBOARDING

In Los Angeles, along the _____ beaches of Santa
VERB ENDING IN "ING"

Monica and Venice, there's an area nicknamed _____ -town,
ANIMAL

where a group of skateboarding _____ known as the
PLURAL NOUN

" _____ -Boys" revolutionized the _____ of
LETTER OF THE ALPHABET   NOUN

skateboarding! Known for their _____ aerial techniques, the
ADJECTIVE

team originally consisted of _____ skateboarders, who would
NUMBER

often _____ in empty pools throughout Southern California.
VERB

There they developed the style known as _____ skateboarding,
ADJECTIVE

which involves riding on an incline or skate _____ , and
NOUN

performing a series of _____ in the air. Many members of
PLURAL NOUN

the team went on to receive _____ -dollar sponsorship deals
NUMBER

from _____ companies looking to _____ in on the
ADJECTIVE   VERB

latest _____ among teenagers. But little did they know that
NOUN

skateboarding was no _____ fad. Because of the
VERB ENDING IN "ING"

Z-Boys, skateboarding is more _____ now than ever before.
ADJECTIVE

MAD LIBS® is fun to play with friends, but you can also play it by yourself! To begin with, DO NOT look at the story on the page below. Fill in the blanks on this page with the words called for. Then, using the words you have selected, fill in the blank spaces in the story.

Now you've created your own hilarious MAD LIBS® game!

USING THE FORCE

VERB _____

NOUN _____

PLURAL NOUN _____

ADJECTIVE _____

ANIMAL _____

TYPE OF CONTAINER _____

SOMETHING ALIVE (PLURAL) _____

NOUN _____

NUMBER _____

ADVERB _____

OCCUPATION _____

NOUN _____

VERB ENDING IN "ING" _____

TYPE OF BUILDING (PLURAL) _____

SILLY WORD _____

NOUN _____

USING THE FORCE

It's hard to _____ it now, but Luke _____-walker
            VERB   NOUN

and *Star* _____ almost never made it to theaters! The
           PLURAL NOUN

_____-wigs at 20th Century _____ had little faith
  ADJECTIVE   ANIMAL

in the project and didn't expect *Star Wars* to perform well at the

_____ office. They thought it was a movie for little
  TYPE OF CONTAINER

_____ and not a/an _____-buster
  SOMETHING ALIVE (PLURAL)   NOUN

worthy of a big weekend release. As a result, the film could only be

seen on _____ screens when it was released on May 25, 1977!
       NUMBER

_____, the film's _____, George Lucas, had
  ADVERB   OCCUPATION

the last _____. Suddenly, moviegoers everywhere began
       NOUN

_____ up outside _____ to witness
  VERB ENDING IN "ING"   TYPE OF BUILDING (PLURAL)

the intergalactic battle between Luke and the movie's antagonist,

Darth _____. Very soon after, the film began to be screened
     SILLY WORD

in thousands of theaters, and everyone was repeating the famous line

"May the _____ be with you!"
       NOUN